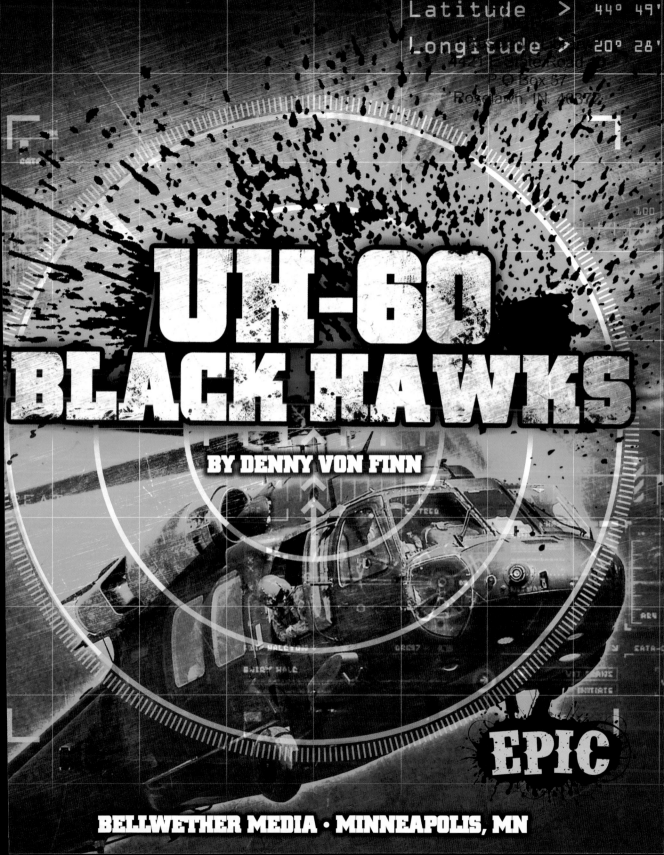

UH-60 BLACK HAWKS

BY DENNY VON FINN

EPIC

BELLWETHER MEDIA · MINNEAPOLIS, MN

EPIC BOOKS are no ordinary books. They burst with intense action, high-speed heroics, and shadows of the unknown. Are you ready for an Epic adventure?

This edition first published in 2013 by Bellwether Media, Inc.

No part of this publication may be reproduced in whole or in part without written permission of the publisher. For information regarding permission, write to Bellwether Media, Inc., Attention: Permissions Department, 5357 Penn Avenue South, Minneapolis, MN 55419.

Library of Congress Cataloging-in-Publication Data

Von Finn, Denny.
UH-60 Black Hawks / by Denny Von Finn.
 p. cm. – (Epic: military vehicles)
 Summary: "Engaging images accompany information about UH-60 Black Hawks. The combination of high-interest subject matter and light text is intended for students in grades 2 through 7"–Provided by publisher.
 Includes bibliographical references and index.
 Audience: Ages 6-12.
 ISBN 978-1-60014-888-0 (hbk. : alk. paper)
 1. Black Hawk (Military transport helicopter)–Juvenile literature. I. Title.
 UG1232.T72.V66 2013
 623.74'65–dc23   2012038168

Printed in the United States of America, North Mankato, MN.

The photographs in this book are reproduced through the courtesy of the United States Department of Defense.
A special thanks to Ted Carlson/Fotodynamics for contributing the photos on pp. 12-13, 18-19, 21.

TABLE OF CONTENTS

UH-60 BLACK HAWKS

A UH-60 Black Hawk **hovers** above a field. Its **rotors** blow dirt into the sky. A **squad** sits inside the Black Hawk.

4

Outside, enemy **rockets** hiss past.
Crew chiefs inside the Black Hawk
fire back. The enemy rockets stop.

Range |++++++++|++++++++|++++++++|
0   50   100

Long ropes fall from the Black Hawk's open doors. Eleven soldiers climb down to the ground. They hit the dirt and rush into battle!

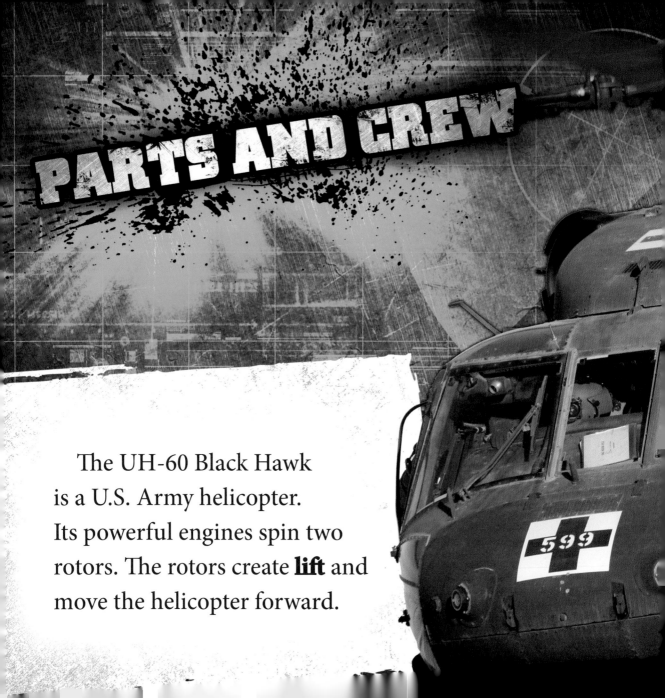

PARTS AND CREW

The UH-60 Black Hawk is a U.S. Army helicopter. Its powerful engines spin two rotors. The rotors create **lift** and move the helicopter forward.

ROTORS

Black Hawk Fact

The UH-60 Black Hawk replaced the UH-1 Huey helicopter in 1979.

Two pilots sit inside the **cockpit** to fly the Black Hawk. **Radar** warns them of enemy weapons.

RADAR

One or two crew chiefs sit behind the cockpit. They provide **cover fire** during dangerous **missions**.

CREW CHIEF

Black Hawk Fact

Black Hawks can be fitted with small wings that carry missiles, rockets, and extra fuel tanks.

UH-60 MISSIONS

Black Hawks perform many missions. They bring troops to dangerous areas. They also help rescue injured soldiers.

Black Hawk Fact

A special Black Hawk known as *Marine One* is used to transport the President of the United States.

There are Black Hawk **variants** for many different tasks. A **stealth** variant was built to sneak up on enemies. It has completed important missions in the **War on Terror**.

VEHICLE BREAKDOWN: UH-60 BLACK HAWK

Used By:	U.S. Army
Entered Service:	1979
Length:	64.8 feet (19.8 meters)
Height:	16.8 feet (5.1 meters)
Rotor Diameter:	53.7 feet (16.4 meters)
Maximum Takeoff Weight:	24,500 pounds (11,113 kilograms)
Top Speed:	183 miles (295 kilometers) per hour
Maximum Range:	1,380 miles (2,220 kilometers)
Ceiling:	19,000 feet (5,790 meters)
Crew:	3 or 4
Weapons:	machine guns, missiles, rockets
Primary Missions:	troop transport, air support, troop rescue

Black Hawks go wherever
there is danger. This makes
them one of the U.S. Army's
most useful weapons.

GLOSSARY

cockpit—the area inside an aircraft where the pilots sit

cover fire—shots fired to distract the enemy from their target; Black Hawk crews use cover fire while they rescue people from dangerous areas.

crew chiefs—crew members who maintain a vehicle and fire its weapons

hovers—stays in one place above the ground

lift—the force that allows a helicopter to rise off the ground

missions—military tasks

radar—a system that uses radio waves to locate targets

rockets—flying explosives that are not guided

rotors—the spinning parts of a helicopter; Black Hawks have a top rotor and a tail rotor.

squad—a small group of soldiers; Black Hawks carry squads of 11 soldiers.

stealth—an aircraft's ability to fly without being spotted by radar

variants—different types of Black Hawks built for different missions

War on Terror—a war led by the United States to stop organized groups from performing acts of violence; the War on Terror began in 2001.

TO LEARN MORE

At the Library

Alvarez, Carlos. *UH-60 Black Hawks*. Minneapolis, Minn.: Bellwether Media, 2011.

Gordon, Nick. *Army Night Stalkers*. Minneapolis, Minn.: Bellwether Media, 2013.

Jackson, Kay. *Military Helicopters in Action*. New York, N.Y.: PowerKids Press, 2009.

On the Web

Learning more about UH-60 Black Hawks is as easy as 1, 2, 3.

1. Go to www.factsurfer.com.

2. Enter "UH-60 Black Hawks" into the search box.

3. Click the "Surf" button and you will see a list of related Web sites.

With factsurfer.com, finding more information is just a click away.

INDEX